THE LITTLE BOOK OF

# KAMALA
# HARRIS

This edition published in 2024 by OH
An Imprint of HEADLINE PUBLISHING GROUP

2

**Disclaimer:**

Cataloguing in Publication Data is available from the British Library

ISBN 978-1-80069-075-2

Compiled and written by: Lisa Dyer
Editorial: Victoria Godden
Designed and typeset in Avenir by: Tony Seddon
Project manager: Russell Porter
Production: Arlene Lestrade
Printed and bound in Canada

MIX
Paper | Supporting
responsible forestry
FSC® C016245

Headline's policy is to use papers that are natural, renewable and recyclable products and made from wood grown in well-managed forests and other controlled sources. The logging and manufacturing processes are expected to conform to the environmental regulations of the country of origin.

HEADLINE PUBLISHING GROUP LIMITED
An Hachette UK Company
Carmelite House, 50 Victoria Embankment, London EC4Y 0DZ

The authorised representative in the EEA is Hachette Ireland, 8 Castlecourt Centre, Castleknock Road, Castleknock, Dublin 15, D15 YF6A, Ireland

www.headline.co.uk   www.hachette.co.uk

# THE LITTLE BOOK OF
# KAMALA HARRIS

## QUOTES TO LIVE BY

# CONTENTS

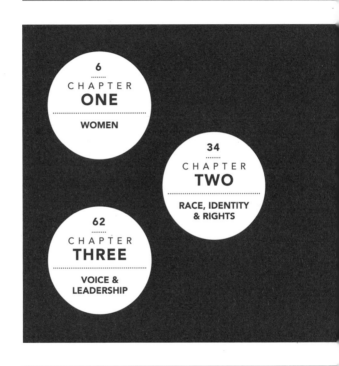

# CHAPTER
# ONE

# WOMEN

On becoming the first woman and the first woman of color to be elected Vice President and presidential nominee, Kamala Harris credited the generations of women on whose shoulders she stood.

By attaining this long-awaited and historic milestone in U.S. politics, she has become an inspiration for women and girls around the world.

But while I may be the first woman in this office, I will not be the last, because every little girl watching tonight sees that this is a country of possibilities.

*Vice President-Elect victory speech, November 7, 2020*

> **"**
> There is nothing more powerful
> than a group of determined
> sisters . . . standing up for what
> we know is right.
> **"**

*The Women's March, Washington, D.C.,*
*January 21, 2017*

What I want young women and girls to know is: You are powerful and your voice matters.

Marie Claire, *February 21, 2019*

If we're not in the room, we
need to speak louder, shout
if we have to . . . because
everyone benefits when
we are heard.

*National Partnership for Women and Families Gala,
Washington, D.C., June 15, 2017*

Simply put, every issue is a Black woman's issue. And Black women's issues are everyone's issues.

*Spelman College, October 26, 2018*

My mother raised my sister and me to be proud, strong Black women, and to be proud of our Indian heritage.

*Democratic National Convention,*
*August 19, 2020*

Women have agency.
Women have value. Women
have authority to make decisions
about their own lives and
their own bodies.

*MSNBC Town Hall, May 28, 2019*

I will fight every day for a woman to make the decision for herself, which means I will respect any woman who decides that is not the decision she wants to make.

*On abortion, MSNBC Town Hall, May 28, 2019*

It is her right. It is her body.
It is her decision.

*Democratic Presidential Debate,*
*October 15, 2019*

When women fought for suffrage, those in power said they were dividing the sexes and disturbing the peace.

*Presidential campaign announcement, January 27, 2019*

And so I'm thinking about [my mother] and about the generations of women—Black women, Asian, white, Latina, and Native American women throughout our nation's history—who have paved the way for this moment tonight. Women who fought and sacrificed so much for equality, liberty, and justice for all.

*Vice President-Elect victory speech, November 7, 2020*

I'm grateful, as the daughter of a mother who raised my sister and me, while working full-time as a scientist in a male-dominated field.

*National Partnership for Women and Families Gala, Washington, D.C., June 15, 2017*

Women have an equal stake in
our future and should have an
equal voice in our politics.

*Twitter, August 21, 2020*

More women should run for office, and more women are running for office, and this is so exciting.

Marie Claire, *February 21, 2019*

Black women and women
of color have long been
underrepresented in elected
office . . . we have an
opportunity to change that. Let's
get to work.

"

*Twitter, August 11, 2020*

... Black women, who are too often overlooked, but so often prove that they are the backbone of our democracy.

*Vice President-Elect victory speech, November 7, 2020*

66

I've been in meetings this year in this city where 10 men will get up and speak before a single woman is called onstage. If you try to tackle the world's problems, you should hear from someone who represents half of the world's population.

99

*Madeleine K. Albright Lunch, Washington, D.C., May 2, 2017*

66

Don't give up . . . We are all,
and should be treated as,
equals, but the disparity in
terms of income and inequality,
for women and women of color,
is significant.

99

Marie Claire, *February 21, 2019*

I have been told many times in my career, 'It's not your time,' 'It's not your turn.' But let me tell you: I eat 'no' for breakfast.

*Twitter, November 2, 2020*

When you walk into every room you ever walk into, do not be burdened by someone else's assumptions of who you are. Do not let anyone ever tell you who you are.

*Spelman College, October 26, 2018*

My mother used to tell me,
'Kamala, you may be the first to
do many things, but make sure
you are not the last.'

*Spelman College, October 26, 2018*

**"**

Tonight, I reflect on their struggle, their determination, and the strength of their vision to see what can be unburdened by what has been. And I stand on their shoulders.

**"**

*In tribute to Black women, Vice President-Elect victory speech, November 7, 2020*

We know that when we help girls learn, we build stronger economies and safer communities.

*Madeleine K. Albright Lunch, Washington, D.C., May 2, 2017*

It's breaking barriers. And when you break things, it hurts. And sometimes you get cut and it can be painful.

*Spelman College, October 26, 2018*

66

[Being the first female, Black, and Asian-American Vice President] helps change the perception . . . And you imagine some young person then seeing, 'Oh, things can be different. I don't have to conform to whatever I'm supposed to do or relegated to do. I can imagine what can be and be unburdened by what has been.'

99

60 Minutes, *October 25, 2020*

---

**"**

And that's why breaking those barriers is worth it. As much as anything else, it is also to create that path for those who will come after us.

**"**

*Spelman College, October 26, 2018*

---

CHAPTER
**TWO**

# RACE, IDENTITY & RIGHTS

As a Black and South-Asian-American female leader in the public eye, Kamala Harris leaned into her identities.

A vocal advocate for racial equality and civil and human rights, from LGBTQ+ to immigration, she has been fearless in addressing hot-button issues in the hopes of creating positive and lasting change.

66

We're experiencing a moral reckoning with racism and systemic injustice that has brought a new coalition of conscience to the streets of our country.

99

*First appearance as the nominee for Vice President, August 12, 2020*

Let's be clear: There is no vaccine for racism. We've gotta do the work. For George Floyd. For Breonna Taylor. For the lives of too many others to name. For our children. For all of us.

*Democratic National Convention, August 19, 2020*

66

# Black Lives Matter is a movement, not a moment.

99

*NowThis News, YouTube, June 30, 2020*

**66**

People of every age and
color and creed who are
finally declaring in one voice:
Black Lives Matter.

**99**

*First appearance as the nominee for*
*Vice President, August 12, 2020*

I always am going to interpret these protests as an essential component of evolution in our country—as an essential component or mark of a real democracy.

*On the BLM protests, NAACP National Convention, September 25, 2020*

66

America and the world are
seeing in vivid detail the
brutality that communities
have known for generations.
You can't deny. You can't look
away. It's there.

99

The New York Times, *June 10, 2020*

No one should have to fear for their life because of their sexuality or color of their skin. We must confront this hate.

*Twitter, January 29, 2019*

And if we care about what happened yesterday in Charlottesville, we've got to care about everyday discrimination as well.

*Facebook, August 13, 2017*

We win when we stand with all of our beautiful diversity, all of our beautiful complexity . . . Young and old, gay and straight, rich and poor, urban and rural, immigrants and native-born, every color of the rainbow.

*California Democratic Convention, May 20, 2017*

How can we defend that our LGBTQ brothers and sisters are treated differently under the law when they walk into their place of work? I will fight for equality.

*CNN Equality Town Hall, October 10, 2019*

To all LGBTQ+ youth who are facing bullying and harassment, know that you deserve to be accepted and loved just as you are.

*Twitter, October 15, 2020*

Vice President-Elect of the United States. Senator, Wife, Momala, Auntie. Fighting for the people. She/her.

*Listing her pronouns on Twitter, November 9, 2020*

It's not niche to be Black
in America.

Washington Post, *September 16, 2019*

---

I'm really sick of having to explain my experiences with racism to people for them to understand that it exists.

The New York Times, *June 10, 2020*

---

There was a little girl in California who was part of the second class to integrate her public schools and who was bused to school every day. And that little girl was me.

*Democratic Presidential Debate,*
*June 27, 2019*

As the only Black person on this
stage, I would like to speak on
the issue of race.

*Democratic Presidential Debate,*
*June 27, 2019*

Racism, sexism, anti-Semitism, homophobia, and transphobia are real in this country. They are age-old forms of hate with new fuel.

*Twitter, July 24, 2019*

**"**

I will tell you that probably over the last 10 years, my white friends would come up to me and say, 'Kamala, what is going on all of a sudden with all this excessive force?' And I would say to them, 'You sound like a colonist.' Because you're seeing it for the first time, you think you've discovered it.

**"**

The New York Times, *June 10, 2020*

66

# In times like this, silence is complicity.

99

*On BLM protests, Cosmopolitan,*
*June 4, 2020*

Justice. Let's talk about that. Because the reality is that the life of a Black person in America has never been treated as fully human.

Elle, *October 6, 2020*

66

There is not a Black man I know, be he a relative, a friend, or a co-worker, who has not been the subject of some form of profiling or discrimination.

99

*Democratic Presidential Debate, June 27, 2019*

66

The time for outrage is now. The time for solidarity is now. The time for action is now. The time for change is now.

99

*On BLM protests, Cosmopolitan, June 4, 2020*

For as long as ours has
been a nation of immigrants,
we have been a nation that
fears immigrants.

The Truths We Hold, *January 8, 2019*

66

This is a nation founded
by immigrants.

99

*MSNBC Town Hall, May 28, 2019*

---

> **"**
> And let's keep up the fight
> for civil rights. Women's
> reproductive rights are at stake,
> LGBT rights are at stake, voting
> rights are at stake.
> **"**

*California Democratic Convention,*
*May 20, 2017*

---

My parents met when they were active in the Civil Rights Movement. I am a daughter of that movement. I grew up knowing about the disparities, inequities, and unfairness . . .

*MSNBC Town Hall, May 28, 2019*

CHAPTER
**THREE**

# VOICE & LEADERSHIP

Unafraid to speak out and stand up, and a longstanding mentor to women seeking public office, Kamala Harris promotes a style of leadership that is based on action.

At each step of her career, she's urged others to dream with ambition and lead with conviction.

66

There will be resistance to your ambition. There will be people who say to you, 'You are out of your lane.' They are burdened by only having the capacity to see what has always been, instead of what can be.

99

*Black Girls Lead 2020 conference,*
*August 1, 2020*

You never have to ask anyone
permission to lead . . . When you
want to lead, you lead.

*Instagram, June 5, 2020*

They will ask us 'What was it like?' And we will tell them, not just how we felt. We will tell them what we did.

*Democratic National Convention, August 19, 2020*

Being undaunted by the fight
means identifying the fight
worth having.

*Spelman College, October 26, 2018*

Dream with ambition, lead with conviction, and see yourselves in a way that others may not, simply because they've never seen it before.

*Vice President-Elect victory speech, November 7, 2020*

Your vote is your voice, and your voice is your power. Don't let anyone take away your power.

*Twitter, November 3, 2020*

It has truly been one of the greatest honors of my life to serve as vice president to our president, Joe Biden. **99**

*First campaign speech as a presidential candidate, July 23, 2024*

The measure of you is so much bigger than you; it's the impact you have. It's what you do in service to others . . . it's about your duty.

*Elle, October 6, 2020*

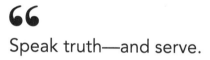

Speak truth—and serve.

*Howard University Commencement Address,*
*May 13, 2017*

KAMALA HARRIS

Because we know when we
organize, mountains move.
When we mobilize, nations
change, and when we vote, we
make history.

The New York Times, *July 27, 2024*

Where deep in your heart you know you can do something, and you may not receive a lot of encouragement, but you must be undaunted. You must be undaunted.

*Spelman College, October 26, 2018*

Do not be burdened by what has been, when you can create what should be.

*University of California, Hastings College of the Law, Commencement Address, April 17, 2018*

# Mr Vice President, I'm speaking. I'm speaking.

*Vice Presidential Debate, October 7, 2020*

Anyone who claims to be a leader must speak like a leader. That means speaking with integrity and truth.

*Instagram, January 2019*

I am not perfect. Lord knows, I am not perfect. But I will always speak with decency and moral clarity and treat all people with dignity and respect.

*Presidential campaign announcement, January 27, 2019*

---

**66**

I was told that I should give up.
I was told that I had no chance.
And I didn't listen.

**99**

*San Francisco State University Commencement*
*Address, May 26, 2007*

---

I am not going to be confined to Donald Trump's definition of who I or anybody else is.

*60 Minutes, October 25, 2020*

I took on perpetrators of all kinds—predators who abused women, fraudsters who ripped off consumers, cheaters who broke the rules for their own gain . . . So, hear me when I say, I know Donald Trump's type.

*First campaign speech as a presidential candidate, Milwaukee, July 23, 2024*

**"**

. . . there are these moments of a crisis that give us the courage and encouragement to try something that actually may be better than how we were doing it before.

**"**

Rolling Stone, *April 16, 2020*

Sometimes to make change you've got to change how change is made.

*Howard University Commencement Address, May 13, 2017*

Doing nothing while the middle class is hurting. That's not leadership. Loose regulations and lax enforcement. That's not leadership.

*Democratic National Convention, September 5, 2012*

If you are fortunate to have opportunity, it is your duty to make sure other people have those opportunities as well.

Marie Claire, *November 6, 2020*

Let's not throw up our hands when it's time to roll up our sleeves. Not now. Not tomorrow. Not ever.

The Truths We Hold, *January 8, 2019*

**"**

I know you will have the
creativity and the independence
to say yes where others have
said no; where others have seen
risk, to see opportunity; and
where others have felt fear, to
find courage.

**"**

*San Francisco State University Commencement
Address, May 26, 2007*

My daily challenge to myself
is to be part of the solution,
to be a joyful warrior in the
battle to come.

The Truths We Hold, *January 8, 2019*

Optimism is the fuel driving every fight I've been in . . . The motivation comes from believing in what can be unburdened by what has been.

Elle, *October 6, 2020*

Speaking the truth means you must speak up and speak out. Even when you're not being asked, and even when it's uncomfortable or inconvenient.

*Howard University Commencement Address, May 13, 2017*

Well Donald, I do hope you'll reconsider to meet me on the debate stage because as the saying goes, if you've if you've got something to say—say it to my face!

*Atlanta rally, July 30, 2024*

66

Today, we face a choice between two very different visions for our nation: one focused on the future, and the other focused on the past. And we are fighting for the future.

99

*Address at the American Federation of Teachers' annual convention, Houston, July 25, 2024*

In the years to come,
what matters most is that we
see ourselves in one another's
struggles.

The Truths We Hold, *January 8, 2019*

When you see something in front of you that's wrong, you can just go ahead and do what you know is right. And it will make a difference.

*Howard University Commencement Address, May 13, 2017*

In this moment, we are in a fight for our most fundamental freedoms, and to this room of leaders, I say, 'Bring it on.'

*Address at the American Federation of Teachers' annual convention, Houston, July 25, 2024*

CHAPTER
**FOUR**

# FAMILY & COMMUNITY

From her love of cooking to her blended family and biracial heritage, Kamala Harris offers a new version of political leadership, one that is relevant, relatable, multicultural, and modern.

I've had a lot of titles over my career, and certainly 'Vice President' will be great. But 'Momala' will always be the one that means the most.

*On her stepchildren's nickname for her,*
*first appearance as the nominee for Vice President,*
*August 12, 2020*

---

**66**

[My mother] taught us to
put family first—the family
you're born into and the family
you choose.

**99**

*Democratic National Convention,*
*August 19, 2020*

---

My mother never sat up and clapped when we did things we were supposed to do. You were supposed to do them, right?

*The Cut, January 8, 2019*

We were raised in a community where we were taught to see a world beyond just ourselves. To be conscious and compassionate about the struggles of all people.

*Democratic National Convention, August 19, 2020*

**❝**

My sister Maya and I were raised by a mother who was all of five feet tall, but if you had ever met her you would have thought she was seven feet tall.

**❞**

*"My Record as a Prosecutor" speech, NAACP Rally, June 8, 2019*

My mother tells the story about how I'm fussing, and she's like, 'Baby, what do you want? What do you need?' And I just looked at her and I said, 'Fweedom.'

Elle, *October 6, 2020*

[My mother would] work all day, then pour her whole heart into Maya and me when she got home. And then after we were fed and in bed, our mother would sit up trying to figure out how to make it all work.

*"Me, Maya, and Mom" political advertisement, August 9, 2019*

66

There was a clarity that came out of my grief and the loss of my mother. About how I saw the world and what my role should be . . .

99

The Cut, *January 8, 2019*

I'm the daughter of a mother who broke down all kinds of barriers. I'm thankful every day to have been raised by her.

*Facebook, May 10, 2020*

Here's the truth people need to understand: To tackle the challenges of the twenty-first century, we must empower women and families. If we do not lift up women and families, everyone will fall short.

*National Partnership for Women and Families Gala, June 15, 2017*

My mother would tell us, 'Don't sit around and complain about things: Do something.' So I did something.

*First appearance as the nominee for Vice President, August 12, 2020*

It's a struggle to consciously work on relationships and on time for yourself. And women have to do that in a way that doesn't make them feel guilty.

Harper's Bazaar, *April 14, 2011*

Surround yourself with really good friends. Have people around you who cheer you on and applaud you and support you and are honest with you, and tell you, you know, when your breath stinks.

Good Morning America *via Twitter, 2019*

I love my husband. He is funny, he is kind, he is patient, he loves my cooking. He's just a really great guy.

*NowThis News, YouTube, 2019*

They are my endless source of love and pure joy . . . my heart wouldn't be whole, nor my life full, without them.

*On her stepchildren, Elle, May 10, 2019*

My mother taught me that service to others gives life purpose and meaning.

*Democratic National Convention,*
*August 19, 2020*

66

Food represents a piece of where we came from and the connections we share.

99

*Twitter, October 28, 2020*

You have to see and smell and feel the circumstances of people to really understand them.

*CBS News, July 30, 2012*

Keep dreaming with ambition and there is nothing you cannot achieve.

*To her step-daughter on her graduation, Elle, August 1, 2024*

66

My mother used to say, 'You don't let people tell you who you are. You tell them who you are.' So that's what I'm gonna do.

99

*NAACP National Convention, September 25, 2020*

66

People who work for me know that family comes first. And I'm fortunate to have a family that is very supportive of the work I do, so I don't have to live two separate lives.

99

*Harper's Bazaar, April 14, 2011*

So seek out mentors, because along the way, none of us, and myself included, has achieved success without people who invested in us.

*Girls Build Leadership Summit,*
*December 15, 2015*

# CHAPTER
## FIVE

# POLITICS & PRINCIPLES

As a prosecutor, she was tough on crime. As a senator, she asked the hard questions and backed progressive legislation. As a presidential candidate, she stands firm in her values.

As the world looks on to see what she has accomplished as Vice President and what else is in store for her future, her integrity, determination, and the ability to rise to a challenge will continue as it has throughout her trailblazing career.

Running for office is similar to being a trial lawyer in a very long trial. It requires adrenaline and stamina; it requires being in shape mentally and emotionally. It's a marathon.

The Daily Beast, *2010*

66

Here's the thing: Every office I've run for I was the first to win. First person of color. First woman. First woman of color. Every time.

99

The New Yorker, *July 22, 2019*

We are going to have to successfully prosecute the case against four more years of Donald Trump and it will take a prosecutor to do it . . . Cuz let's think about it, dude's gotta go. Dude's gotta go.

*Iowa Democratic Steak Fry campaign speech, September 21, 2019*

We have foreign powers
infecting the White House
like malware.

*Presidential campaign announcement,*
*January 27, 2019*

If someone is trying to suppress our vote, then we will vote them out of office.

*Spelman College, October 26, 2018*

66

To be sure, we've won and
we've lost, but we've never
stopped fighting.

99

*Presidential campaign announcement,*
*January 27, 2019*

# 66
# We did it. We did it, Joe!

# 99

*Kamala Harris speaks to Joe Biden after winning the*
*2020 Election, Twitter, November 7, 2020*

66

You marched and organized for equality and justice. For our lives, and for our planet. And then you voted. You delivered a clear message. You chose hope, unity, decency, science, and, yes, truth.

99

*Vice President-Elect victory speech, November 7, 2020*

Politics is a realm where
the grand pronouncement
often takes the place of the
painstaking and detail-oriented
work of getting meaningful
things done.

The Truths We Hold, *January 8, 2019*

66

I'll be judged on the body of
work and not the popularity
of any one decision.

99

East Bay Times, *April 2015*

In every work environment, there will be politics. If you really want to rise to the top, you need to figure out what those politics in your workplace are. Then, you hook it in.

Elle + Lenny, *October 23, 2015*

Don't pretend that you can just be oblivious to politics. You can't. What you never do is break your personal code.

Elle + Lenny, *October 23, 2015*

Throughout all of the recent events and the emotional rollercoaster our country has been on, we cannot lose hope. And in order to have hope, one must first speak truth.

*Cosmopolitan, June 4, 2020*

66

# Seek truth, speak truth, and fight for the truth.

99

*Presidential campaign announcement,*
*January 27, 2019*

I am a voice for the voiceless, and that's what I've always wanted to be.

Harper's Bazaar, *April 14, 2011*

> **"**
> At every step of the way, I've
> been guided by the words I
> spoke from the first time I stood
> in a courtroom: 'Kamala Harris,
> For the People.'
> **"**

*Democratic National Convention,*
*August 19, 2020*

You are not invisible. We all stand together. That's the power of the people.

*Presidential campaign announcement, January 27, 2019*

'The People' means all of us.
It means that when someone
commits a crime against any one
of us, it is a crime against all of
us . . . the community is harmed
when you are harmed.

*UCLA Law School Commencement Address,
May 13, 2009*

Standing up for the people means fighting for children, even though they don't write the big checks or have the fanciest lobbyist.

*Californian Democratic Convention, May 16, 2015*

I'm opposed to any policy that would deny, in our country, any human being from access to public safety, public education, or public health, period.

*CNN, State of the Union, May 12, 2019*

66

# The economy is not working for working people.

99

*Spelman College, October 26, 2018*

**❝**

Now is when the real work begins. The hard work. The necessary work. The good work. . . . To rebuild our economy so it works for working people. To root out systemic racism in our justice system and society. To combat the climate crisis. To unite our country and heal the soul of our nation.

**❞**

*Vice President-Elect victory speech, November 7, 2020*

66

We have to act with fierce urgency. Justice demands it.

99

The Truths We Hold, *January 8, 2019*

66

[Justice] is not about
benevolence or charity; it is
about every human being's
God-given right.

99

Elle, *October 6, 2020*

---

**"**

Donald Trump doesn't
understand the presidency.
He thinks it's all about him.
Well, it's not. It's about you . . .
The People.

**"**

*Remarks in advance of the Republican National*
*Convention, August 27, 2020*

---

**"**

I went after transnational gangs, drug cartels and human traffickers that came into our country illegally. I prosecuted them in case after case, and I won. Donald Trump, on the other hand, has been talking a big game about securing our border, but he does not walk the walk.

**"**

*Atlanta rally, July 30, 2024*

Make no mistake, the road ahead will not be easy. We will stumble. We may fall short. But I pledge to you that we will act boldly and deal with our challenges honestly.

*Democratic National Convention, August 19, 2020*

Joe and I have a lot in common, and one of them is that we don't back down from a good fight if it's a fight worth having.

San Francisco Chronicle, *September 11, 2020*

I'll tell you, sitting across
the table from the big banks,
I witnessed the arrogance
of power. Wealthy bankers
accusing innocent homeowners
of fault, as if Wall Street's mess
was of the people's making.

*Presidential campaign announcement,*
*January 27, 2019*

As an attorney general, I held big Wall Street banks accountable for fraud. Donald Trump was found guilty of fraud. In this campaign, I will proudly put my record against his any day, including on the issue of immigration.

*Atlanta rally, July 30, 2024*

I am a prosecutor in my bones.
When I see something,
I immediately go to: How is
this going to affect a child?

Elle + Lenny, *October 23, 2015*

I've fought for children, and survivors of sexual assault. I've fought against transnational gangs. I took on the biggest banks and helped take down one of the biggest for-profit colleges. I know a predator when I see one.

*Democratic National Convention, August 19, 2020*

I believe that a child going
without an education is
tantamount to a crime.

*Commonwealth Club speech,*
*January 14, 2010*

66

I know what a crime looks like. I will tell you: An undocumented immigrant is not a criminal.

99

*Senate speech, February 16, 2017*

You can want the police to stop crime in your neighborhood and also want them to stop using excessive force. You can want them to hunt down a killer on your streets and also want them to stop using racial profiling.

The Truths We Hold, *January 8, 2019*

# 66
# Bad cops are bad for good cops.
**99**

*On police reform, NAACP National Convention,*
*September 5, 2020*

When we have an equal number of representatives in Congress —equal number meaning representative of who the population is as a whole—we will be better and stronger.

Marie Claire, *February 21, 2019*

America has tried these failed
policies, and we are not going
back—we're not going back.

Atlanta rally, July 30, 2024

# CHAPTER
## SIX

# AMERICA

As a child of parents born in India and Jamaica, Kamala Harris's back story is the American story.

She has spoken passionately about the country as a land founded by immigrants, where a shared struggle and purpose is united in a shared vision, where opportunity and hard work bring achievement.

---

Democracy cannot flourish amid fear. Liberty cannot bloom amid hate. Justice cannot take root amid rage.

*The Truths We Hold, January 8, 2019*

---

---

America's democracy is not
guaranteed. It is only as strong
as our willingness to fight
for it.

99

*Vice President-Elect victory speech,*
*November 7, 2020*

---

Let's speak truth here today —this president isn't trying to make America great; he's trying to make America hate.

*On Donald Trump, Politico, May 5, 2019*

Let's fight with conviction. Let's fight with hope. Let's fight with confidence in ourselves, and a commitment to each other —to the America we know is possible, the America we love.

*Democratic National Convention, August 19, 2020*

You think you just fell out of a coconut tree? You exist in the context of all in which you live and what came before you.

*Remark at a White House event that went viral after Harris began her presidential campaign\*, May 10, 2023.*

*\* Her bid was dubbed "Operation Coconut Tree".*

Imperfect though we may be,
I believe we are a great country.
And part of what makes us great
are our democratic institutions
that protect our fundamental
ideals—freedom of religion and
the rule of law, protection from
discrimination based on national
origin, freedom of the press, and
a 200-year history as a nation
built by immigrants.

*Senate speech, February 16, 2017*

America is always strongest when we lead with our values . . . Equal protection, the right to marry anyone you love, and the right to control our reproductive healthcare decisions and our own bodies.

*California Democratic Convention, May 16, 2015*

Americans are united by their
aspirations—for themselves and
their families.

*Twitter, December 2, 2020*

We are a great country and
part of what makes us great
is fighting for our ideals . . .
that we are all and should
be treated as equals.

*Senator-Elect victory speech,*
*November 8, 2016*

People in power are trying to convince us that the villain in our American story is each other. But that is not our story. That is not who we are. That's not our America.

*Presidential campaign announcement, January 27, 2019*

To everyone keeping up the fight, you are doing something. You are the reason I know we are going to bring our country closer to realizing its great promise.

*First appearance as the nominee for Vice President, August 12, 2020*

We were founded on noble ideals. The ideals that were present when we wrote the Constitution of the United States and all of its amendments and the Bill of Rights and Declaration of Independence. We said you are equal and should be treated that way.

*MSNBC Town Hall, May 28, 2019*

We are a nation that, at its best, loves, protects, and helps our fellow Americans.

*Remarks in advance of the Republican National Convention, August 27, 2020*

You respect the American people when you tell them the truth.

*Vice Presidential Debate, October 7, 2020*

We, The People, have the power to build a better future.

*Vice President-Elect victory speech, November 7, 2020*

Our country's wounds can be healed. We just have to have the political courage to act.

Cosmopolitan, *June 4, 2020*

A patriot is not someone who condones the conduct of our country whatever it does. It is someone who fights every day for the ideals of the country, whatever it takes.

*The Truths We Hold, January 8, 2019*

Our unity is our strength, and our diversity is our power. We reject the myth of 'us' vs. 'them'. We are in this together.

*Twitter, July 21, 2016*

66

We have to remember the shoulders on which we stand—generations of Americans before us led the fight for freedom. And now . . . the baton is in our hands.

99

*First campaign speech as a presidential candidate, Milwaukee, July 23, 2024*

We must dissent from the indifference. We must dissent from the apathy. We must dissent from the fear, the hatred, and the mistrust.

The Truths We Hold, *January 8, 2019*

66

What I hope and pray is that
we can get to a point where,
through what are undoubtedly
difficult conversations, we
confront the real history of
America. Doing it in a way that
is motivated by love, but also
is fully honest.

99

Elle, *October 6, 2020*

We all have so much more
in common than what
separates us.

*Presidential campaign announcement,*
*January 27, 2019*

Our democracy is at its
strongest and most powerful
when everyone participates.

*MSNBC Town Hall, May 28, 2019*

---

I'll fight for an America where
we keep our word and where
we honor our promises. Because
that's our America.

*Presidential campaign announcement,*
*January 27, 2019*

---

This is a fight that is not only for the soul of our country, this is a fight born out of love of country.

*Iowa State Fair campaign speech,*
*August 10, 2019*

**"**

[I am] committed to a vision of our nation as a beloved community where all are welcome no matter what we look like, no matter where we come from or who we love.

**"**

*Democratic National Convention,*
*August 19, 2020*

It can't be about looking at yesterday; we need to be focused on tomorrow.

*Liberty and Justice Dinner, Iowa, November 1, 2019*

66

What can be, unburdened by
what has been.

99

*Twitter, 2020*

We are aspirational. We are also clear-eyed. We've not yet reached those ideals . . . And so fight we will and fight we must.

*Iowa State Fair campaign speech, August 10, 2019*

66

When [my mother] came here
from India at the age of 19,
maybe she didn't quite imagine
this moment. But she believed
so deeply in an America where a
moment like this is possible.

99

*Vice President-Elect victory speech,*
*November 7, 2020*

---

The American Dream belongs
to all of us.

*Democratic National Convention,*
*September 5, 2012*

---